GW00646264

JESUS
THE LIVING LORD

MICHAEL RAMSEY

SLG Press
Convent of the Incarnation
Fairacres Oxford

ISBN 0 7283 01326

ISSN 0307-1405

Printed by Will Print Oxford England

ACKNOWLEDGEMENT

This lecture, given in Canterbury Cathedral on 2 November 1966, is reprinted by permission of the Dean and Chapter of Canterbury.

OUR SUBJECT tonight is 'Jesus, the Living Lord'. Jesus lived nearly two thousand years ago. Secular history of the time records that he was a prophet and teacher in Palestine; he founded a sect, and he was put to death by crucifixion. Christians claim that Jesus is alive now and matters tremendously still for the human race; but those who are not Christians are very puzzled by this claim, and indeed think it ridiculous. The claim that Jesus is alive now and matters very much is entirely familiar to us Christians, but it is well that we should step back a few paces and ask how this is so. And that is what I ask you to do tonight.

We begin with a picture of what Jesus did and taught when he lived in Palestine. For the purpose of this initial picture, I take the Gospel of Mark—the first of the Gospels to be written—and I take also the records shared in common in Matthew's Gospel and Luke's Gospel. For the moment I leave on one side the Gospel that bears the name of John, for though I believe that that Gospel contains very reliable history, it was written a good deal later than the others and gives something of a reinterpretation of the picture of Jesus. Now what is the original picture? On the soil of Palestine there suddenly appears Jesus, a prophet and teacher, and like the prophets of old he has as his great theme the Kingdom of God. What did that mean? The Kingdom of God in biblical thought and language meant God's sovereignty or reign, and when prophets and psalmists spoke of 'the Kingdom' they were speaking of God's sovereignty or reign as an eternal fact in the universe, and this sovereignty or reign is one day to be realised and accepted on earth, making thus a profound difference to the whole life of the world. Like the prophets of old, Jesus proclaims the Kingdom of God; but unlike them, he proclaims it as something coming imminently—coming so soon that indeed it is already here. 'Here is the Kingdom of God,' is his message. 'Believe that this is so, receive it, enter it,

1

obey it.' Jesus came into Galilee saying, 'The time is fulfilled. The reign of God is at hand. Repent and believe in the good news.'

Now Jesus shows the presence of the Kingdom of God in two principal ways. The first way is his mighty works. Often in the narratives we read about his mighty works. Those mighty works are described as miraculous, and there are a host of questions we can ask about their character and their credibility. But forgive me for concentrating now on one point: the meaning of these mighty works in the story as we have it, their place in the story and their relation to the Kingdom of God which Jesus is proclaiming. These works include healing the sick, curing people with diseases, giving sight to the blind, giving hearing to the deaf and driving out demons which possess unfortunate people and torment their lives. And these works of Jesus assert the sovereignty of God in the whole range of human life. These unhappy phenomena are contrary to God's reign, and God's reign means their conquest. Thus Jesus sets forth the reign of God as the purpose of God being accomplished in the whole range of the life of man, bodily as well as spiritual. And for a time these great works of healing and other works are immensely popular. The people crowd around Jesus and look to him as a great popular healer, thronging him, but we find Jesus often withdrawing from the crowds; though he does so much healing he is unwilling to let himself be regarded just as a popular healer. And why? Because the works of healing are only a part of the programme of the Kingdom of God, and the Kingdom of God means the bringing of the whole of life into conformity with God's will and purpose; and that which is most contrary to God's will and purpose is the distorted wills of men, diseased by selfishness and sin, and acting in ways utterly destructive of the divine righteousness. As we see this total programme of the Kingdom of God we realise that in the mind of Jesus the bodily health of man, though so very important, is not an end in itself; it is but one part of the life of man which exists to do God's will and reflect his righteousness and his love. So, while one aspect of the works of the Kingdom is very popular to the hearers and see-ers of Jesus, the central meaning of the Kingdom is far from popular because it means the bringing of sinful human wills into conformity with the supreme righteousness of God. Thus we find Jesus, as the story proceeds, more and more withdrawing from his work of healing, even though it is a work so utterly near to his heart, and concentrating upon the paramount theme of sin and the forgiveness of sin. And it is in the realm of sin and forgiveness and the establishment of righteousness that the central core of the reign of God is going to be established.

This brings us to the second way in which Jesus set forth the Kingdom, the reign of God. The first way is mighty works; the second way is teaching of righteousness. How many of the pages of the Gospels are filled with this teaching of a new righteousness. And we notice that while the righteousness taught by Jesus is not primarily a code of rules, it does indeed include divine law. Divine law is not abolished by Jesus; far from it. Divine law is fulfilled and deepened, and if we are faithful to the teaching of Jesus we know that divine law has still a very central place in the righteousness of the Kingdom of God. But the heart of the ethics of Jesus is not in law, it is in a relationship of men and women and children to God. They are to live towards God, live with the sensitive side of their being turned towards God; and in this being near to God, in trusting him and loving him, they will find themselves reflecting his character, being possessed by his rule; and that means living as citizens of the Kingdom of God. It is the ethics of a God relationship. For instance, men are to love their enemies. Why? How? Because God's providential goodness is quite indiscriminate. He gives sunshine and he gives rain indiscriminately to all of us, the good and the bad alike, and if we are utterly near to God we shall just find ourselves reflecting this indiscriminate love of his and love our enemies as well as our friends. Again, one of the evils in human life is fear, and fear springing from lack of trust is the soil in which so much self-concern and protective selfishness grows. But live near to God, rejoicing in God's providential care, and you won't worry, you won't fear, you will be every hour and every minute in the presence of God who cares for the lilies and clothes the grass and cares infinitely for you. That habitual nearness to God and trust in his providence will remove fear from your life; and being without fear you will be without those horrid sins that have fear as their root.

Again, God forgives all of us, however terrible our behaviour may have been, however undeserving of God's forgiveness we may be. God has forgiven us so much that living near to God within God's Kingdom or reign we shall find ourselves forgiving others instead of being resentful towards them, because we are just reflecting the nearness of God towards whom our lives are being lived. Such is the righteousness of a Godward relationship, and this righteousness of a Godward relationship is rooted in the attitude of childlike dependence and receptivity towards God. Now in many ways the ethical teaching of Jesus is terribly hard, and sometimes it is terribly hard because Jesus gives such stern calls to sacrifice and renunciation, though sacrifice and renunciation is, in the teaching of Jesus, so very joyful if it is just a part of this nearness to God and God himself is our constant reward. But the greatest difficulty in the ethical teaching of Jesus is not, I would say, his stern calls to renunciation nearly so much as his insistence on the generosity of God's giving to us, demanding that we shall be utterly humble, utterly childlike, utterly receptive. It is this dependence, humility, receptivity, childlikeness that is the hard thing that Jesus demands that we shall follow; that we shall be humble enough to receive a goodness, a righteousness that is all God's gift and is never our achievement. Such is the righteousness of the Kingdom of God, a righteousness which Jesus describes sometimes as entering the Kingdom, sometimes as receiving the Kingdom, and always as obeying because the word Kingdom itself means God ruling in human hearts and wills.

Now we can't, alas, follow tonight more fully the theme of the works of Jesus or the theme of the righteousness of the Kingdom, and I ask you to concentrate just on this point: that the theme of Jesus in his mission is the Kingdom of God. In our earliest records he appears as serving the Kingdom, absorbed in the Kingdom and in his heavenly Father whose Kingdom it is; and thus not absorbed in his own claims, not primarily dwelling upon himself and his own claims because it is the Kingdom that is his theme. He effaces himself in proclaiming and serving God's Kingdom. Now it is in the midst of this self-effacement of Jesus, whose theme is not himself but the Kingdom, that we realise how stupendous the implied claims of Jesus are. Think of some of these implied claims. They imply that somehow the coming of the Kingdom hinges upon himself and his own presence in the world, so that men's dealings with him are the key to their nearness to the Kingdom. For instance, men must be ready to take up their crosses and suffer and lose their lives in order to win them. Why? For what? 'For my sake,' says Jesus. It is a personal allegiance to him; doing it for him. The implied claim is stupendous. Here is another instance; it is from the Sermon on the Mount: 'At the final judgement all men are going to be judged.' And if they have been unfaithful to the righteousness of the Kingdom there will be a very painful rejection. What will that rejection mean? It will be Jesus saying to them, 'Depart from me. I never knew you.' In the final judgement it will be the personal relation to Jesus himself that will be the issue, and it will be rejection by Jesus from the presence of Jesus that may be the terrible thing.

Another instance: there is going to be at the heart of the Kingdom of God a new covenant, and a new covenant means a new total relationship between God and the human race, a relationship in which God's law is written in men's hearts and their sins are forgiven; a new bond between God and humanity. 'And', says Jesus—and he is speaking at the Last Supper—'that bond, that covenant, will be the new covenant in my blood.' It will all turn upon the death of Jesus on the cross. What a stupendous claim that is.

And then there is an implied claim which peeps out, perhaps greater than any of these, and it is this: again and again Jesus insists that all men must repent, all men must pray, 'forgive us our sins '; and forgiveness is among the great gifts which Jesus brings. Now throughout religious history the most saintly men and saintly prophets and teachers have themselves been aware of their own sins and conscience-stricken about them, and join in with their people in asking for God's forgiveness. But not so Jesus. While he insists upon the universal repentance of all people, there is never on his own lips the language of repentance, because quietly, unobtrusively, he is himself the very source of that righteousness which is the gift of God. The implications of that are just tremendous—Jesus, not a fellow-sinner with ourselves, but Jesus who is himself the source, the embodiment of that righteousness; Jesus who can say, taking upon himself the very language used of the divine wisdom in the older literature, 'Come unto me and I will give you rest.'

Now these claims imply that Jesus has a special place himself in the coming of the Kingdom. The Kingdom is in a wonderful way embodied in himself and in his own person. Where he is, there is God's reign; and being with him and accepting him is accepting God's reign. He is indeed as the very gate into the Kingdom of God, through whom and in whom we enter it. And how did Jesus publicly express these claims? Was he the Messiah whom the Jews expected? When

Simon Peter at Caesarea Philippi, asked by Jesus who he thought he was, acknowledged that Jesus was the Messiah, Jesus accepted the title because it was true, but at once explained that while he was Messiah he was Messiah with a very great difference because he was a Messiah whose reign was going to come through suffering and death. Now often in his public teaching Jesus designated himself the Son of Man; and the title Son of Man, used so often by Jesus, was perhaps deliberately provocative and challenging. On the one hand it meant that he was identifying himself with humanity; he was the representative man, summing up humanity in himself. But when we read the seventh chapter of the Book of Daniel we see the term 'Son of Man' used of a future coming on the clouds in the glory of heaven. Thus when Jesus spoke of himself as 'Son of Man', he was speaking both of his representative manhood and also of a future glorious triumph that was going to come. In speaking to the disciples Jesus mentioned the underlying secret of his person, and that underlying secret was a unique Sonship possessed by him in relation to God the Father. Let me read the very striking words from St Matthew 11:27, words also parallelled in the Gospel of St Luke: 'All things are delivered unto me of my Father; and no-one knoweth the Son save the Father, neither doth any know the Father save the Son and he to whom the Son will reveal him.' There is a claim to a unique Sonship, meaning a deep intimacy with God, an intimacy including a perfect knowledge of God and ability to reveal God to whomsoever he will.

Now these claims made by Jesus, partly in private teaching to the disciples and partly in mysterious hints and challenges in his public teaching, and always in the originality of his teaching and his claims concerning the Kingdom, caused intense resentment. A most unusual thing happened. The two great parties in the country—the party of the Saducees, the followers of the very worldly high priests, and the party of the Pharisees, which was the godly party of the teachers of the law, parties normally estranged and at daggers drawn, for once combined; and what led them to combine was their desire to destroy Jesus. And because of the plot to destroy Jesus, and because of the awareness of Jesus that this plot existed and that if he persisted in his immediate course death inevitably awaited him, a dark shadow falls across the story, and Jesus, from the event in Caesarea Philippi onwards, begins to teach the disciples that he must die. Now there appears the most amazing thing that we have yet seen in the story. This coming death of Jesus is not in the mind of Jesus a terrible setback or a defeat, a triumph of ungodliness. No, it is something which God in his purpose is going to use, and use in such a way that the death by crucifixion will in itself be a mighty means of the coming of the consummation of the Kingdom of God breaking into the world. It might be thought that the coming tragedy meant that the mighty works of Jesus were fatally interrupted and abandoned. No. His death by crucifixion is going to be turned into a work mightier in its effects than all the works we have been thinking about. It might be thought that the righteousness of the Kingdom would be utterly contradicted by this dreadful death. But no. The death by crucifixion is going to be the greatest showing forth of divine righteousness in action. Finally, it might be thought that the Kingdom or reign of God would be utterly contradicted and frustrated by this tragedy. But on the contrary, it is in the cross that the reign of God is going to be superbly seen.

So Jesus, on the way to Jerusalem, teaches the disciples that his death on Calvary is going to be on his part a great act of serving, of ministering to the human race for the defeat of sin and the redemption of suffering; and at the Last Supper he tells them that it is going to be the basis of a new covenant relationship, a new intimate bond between God and the human race for members of the human race to receive, accept and enter upon if they will.

Jesus died by crucifixion on the Friday. A few days later it was the conviction of the apostles that Jesus was alive, and in the conviction that Jesus was alive they presently faced the people in the city of Jerusalem, still proclaiming the Kingdom of God which Jesus had proclaimed, but now proclaiming that the crucifixion of Jesus and his raising from the dead were the vindication of the Kingdom; that the people were called upon to believe this good news, to repent of their sins, and to be received into fellowship with God on the basis of this repentance. Now clearly something had happened to change the body of disciples from being a band defeated and scattered into being a united body confidently facing the world with the proclamation of the Gospel of Jesus. Something must have happened. The historian who does not accept the resurrection is, I think, in a very difficult predicament to account for what happened, because it must have been either fraud or delusion; and it seems, simply from the point of view of scientific history, very hard to maintain that the subsequent lives of the apostolic company had no more than fraud or delusion as their basis. The Church's belief that Jesus had been raised from death was supported by evidence and the evidence was and is of three kinds. First, the fact of the Church itself restored to life again. Second, the evidence that the apostles and others had seen Jesus alive from death and had had through seeing and hearing a vivid convincing personal impact of his presence—though it was authentically his presence it was in a form so new that the language of seeing him and hearing him had very new ways about it. And the third evidence was that some of the women and apostles themselves found the tomb empty. It is important to notice that the evidence included, and includes, those three elements. It is clear that in the first age of Christianity there were those to whom one part of the evidence mattered more than other parts. There are today those to whom one part of the evidence matters more and is more compelling than other parts. But in the total testimony of the Church in the first stage and in the total testimony of the Church down the ages, each of those three parts of the evidence has its great place and value: the mere fact of the existence of the Church, the evidence of the appearances, and the evidence of the empty tomb.

But I must press on, because we want now to see what was the belief concerning Jesus which emerged from this. During his life on earth they have been devoted disciples and followers; they have not yet become worshippers. After the resurrection and the ascension—and the ascension was something which happened; they saw Jesus received into a cloud and disappear from sight. It happened, but it happened as the symbol to them of the fact that Jesus now shared in the divine sovereignty and that the presence and power of Jesus were accessible anywhere and everywhere. They knew right well that the ascension did not mean that Jesus had gone to be located in some particular locality beyond the skies. No, they knew well enough that to be ascended at the right hand of God meant to share in God's omnipresence, to share in a new mode of being accessible to believers at any time and in any place hereafter—after the resurrection and the ascension, the disciples and their fellow first Christians became worshippers of Jesus. Their attitude toward him passed beyond the disciples of a teacher, beyond the ardent devotees of a leader, into worshipping one whom they believed to be divine. The impact of Jesus upon them, through their knowledge of him in his moral claim, his life, his death and his rising again, was such that they could not withhold from him the worship and adoration which are due to deity alone. And it is here that the distinctive doctrine of Christianity explicitly comes in sight: the divinity of Jesus Christ. The doctrine, you see, did not begin in theory or speculation, it began in their experience of Jesus and the impact of Jesus upon them. And it is all the more striking that these men were Jewish monotheists, believers in one God to whom the idea of more than one God was incredible and blasphemous; and yet within the belief in one God, to which they still adhered, they ascribed deity to Jesus as the total embodiment of God towards men in their experience. This belief, first expressed in an attitude of worship, called for language and imagery in which to express it, and a variety of language and imagery was used. Thus, 'Jesus is the unique Son of God', 'Jesus is light of light', 'Jesus is the image of the unseen God', 'He that hath seen me hath seen the Father'. All these images express all too inadequately the worshipfulness of Jesus as divine.

I want to end by recalling you to one very significant piece of imagery used about him in the early Church. It is the imagery used by St John in the prologue of his Gospel. Now the great thing about the Gospel of John is this: that though, as I have said already, I believe it contains authentic historical records, it is also written from the point of view of one seeing the events rather from a distance; and he is asking not just what was the impression that this made upon us at the time, but what is the total impression of this for the human race. What does it all mean for humanity down the ages? That is the question in St John's mind, and it is in terms of that question that he told that story.

Well, what *does* it mean for humanity all down the ages? 'The Word became flesh and dwelt among us and we beheld—we saw—His glory.' Now that is terribly familiar—the Gospel every Christmas Day. But step back and look at what an astonishing statement it is. 'Word', 'flesh', both are biblical terms with a very distinct meaning. 'Word': that denotes One who is living, active, Creator divine. 'The Word of the Lord lasts for ever.' It speaks of divine creativity. 'By the Word of the Lord were the heavens made.' The very divine voice itself. 'Flesh': that, as a biblical term, denotes the opposite. Flesh means that which is mortal, frail, perishing, destined to die. 'All flesh is as grass.' Now the contrast is between one who is divine with sharing the divine life of the Creator himself—the Living One—and human life viewed in all its creatureliness and frailty and mortality, and St John says this: that looking at the whole story of Jesus, the teaching, the life, the death, the resurrection, and asking what its total meaning is, the total meaning is that in this happening the Word became flesh; one who is divine took upon himself genuinely our frail, creaturely human existence. Was that credible? The more sophisticated people in the world mocked and thought it incredible. Is it credible to us? I think if we dare to say we believe it we must first face what a hard paradox it is and realise what a paradox it is. But we are aided to believe it to be really credible if we go on to the words of St John which follow. 'The Word became flesh and dwelt among us and we beheld his glory.' Now 'glory' in the Bible means splendour, the splendour of God. But in the Gospel of St John we see again and again that the divine splendour means his self-giving love, the divine power of giving himself utterly in sacrifice and self-effacement; and this power of self-effacing, sacrificial, self-giving love—that is the very essence of the character of God. And because that is the very essence of the character of God, God is going to be capable of an act of self-giving love going far beyond all the analogies of self-giving love with which we ourselves are familiar; and that, St John tells us, is what happened in this act of self-giving love. 'The Word became flesh', and that act was itself the divine glory. Then St John, drawing out the total meaning of the total event, goes on to tell the story as the showing forth of the divine glory. The story in St John is essentially the same story as the story told in the earlier Gospels, but again and again its everlasting meaning is being brought out in the language which is being used; and the most significant language is this language of glory, and the glory of Christ is this total self-giving, self-effacing love, disclosing on earth the total self-giving, self-effacing love of the Godhead. And as the earlier Gospels showed us, the crucifixion was not a contradiction of the Kingdom; but no, it belonged to the Kingdom; it does not contradict the glory. The crucifixion is in itself the greatest showing forth of the glory, and we can thus write under the picture of the Passion, no less than under the picture of Bethlehem, 'We saw his glory'.

One more point: St John shows us that the glory was revealed in Jesus not that it should end there, but that it should be passed on from Jesus to those who accept him through the ministrations of the Church. In the prayer of the Last Supper on the night before Calvary, Jesus prays that he may glorify the Father, that the Father may glorify him, and that the glory may be given to the apostles and to all subsequent Christian believers as a gift. He says, 'Father, the glory thou gavest me I have given to them.' And the significance of Jesus is able to be summed up thus: Jesus in his life and teaching and death and resurrection was the very embodiment of the Kingdom of God, the reign of God in the world, to use the language of his own teaching and the language of the first three Gospels. In the language of the Fourth Gospel Jesus, in this same teaching and life and death and resurrection, was the showing to the world of the divine glory. The Kingdom continues through the Lordship of the risen Jesus, and it is for us utterly to enter the Kingdom, receive it and live by it and to draw others to share in it. Equally, the glory of Jesus in his risen life lives on, and it is for us to receive his gift of glory, make it our own and live by it: the glory is nothing less than that self-effacing, sacrificial love which was the essence of the life of Jesus himself and is meant to become the essence of those who accept him and who live by him. And just as, if we think in terms of the

Kingdom there is the conflict still raging between the Kingdom of God and the rebelliousness of selfish human wills, so in terms of glory there is the conflict raging between the glory of God which is self-giving love and the glory of man which is man's self-aggrandisement. The significance of Jesus for the world is that he has revealed the nature of this conflict and revealed the victorious power by which the conflict may be won.

'Jesus is Lord.' That was and is the central credal affirmation. 'Jesus': that means that we believe in the historic life of a person two thousand years ago. 'Is': that means that Jesus is of the present as well as the past: he is; he is still. And, 'Lord': to say that means that we confess his deity as the early believers confessed his deity, and the confession of his deity is not only the expression of our intellectual belief, but it is also the expression of a moral allegiance: to say that Jesus is Lord means that we acknowledge that he, and he alone, must rule our motives, our actions and our lives.